It's a Beautiful Day with MISTER ROGERS®

Arranged by Phillip Keveren

ISBN 978-1-5400-6750-0

Visit Hal Leonard Online at
www.halleonard.com

Contact us:
Hal Leonard
7777 West Bluemound Road
Milwaukee, WI 53213
Email: info@halleonard.com

In Europe, contact:
Hal Leonard Europe Limited
42 Wigmore Street
Marylebone, London, W1U 2RN
Email: info@halleonardeurope.com

In Australia, contact:
Hal Leonard Australia Pty. Ltd.
4 Lentara Court
Cheltenham, Victoria, 3192 Australia
Email: info@halleonard.com.au

"Music is so much a part of me.
Throughout my life, I have learned what
music can mean in expressing the full range
of feelings I want to share."

—Fred Rogers

Are You Brave?

(From "MISTER ROGERS' NEIGHBORHOOD")

Words and Music by
Fred Rogers

Are you brave and don't

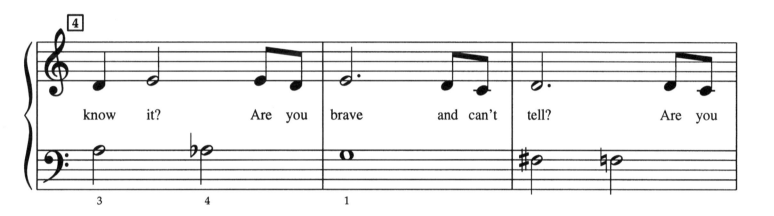

know it? Are you brave and can't tell? Are you

Duet Part (Student plays one octave higher.)

With pedal

brave and just don't know it while oth-ers know it ver - y

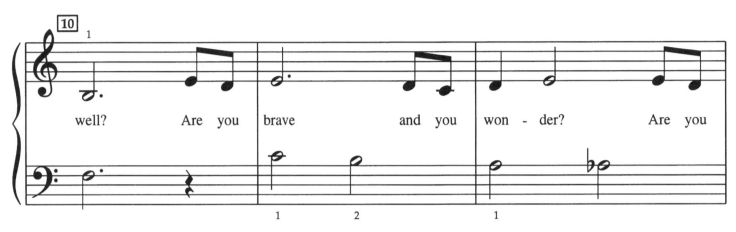

well? Are you brave and you won - der? Are you

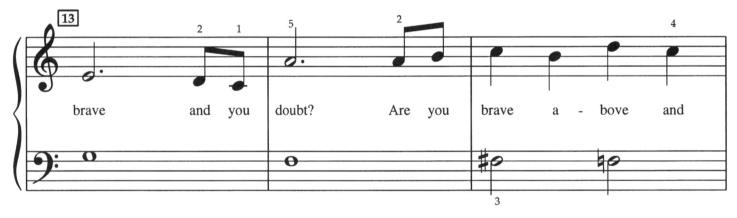

brave and you doubt? Are you brave a - bove and

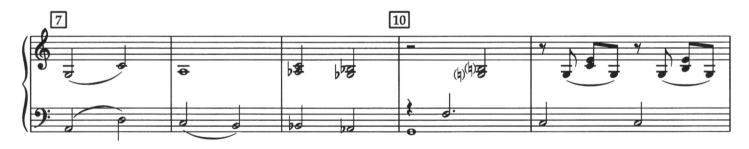

4

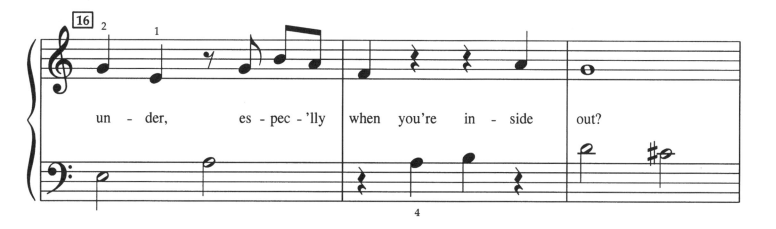

un - der, es - pec - 'lly when you're in - side out?

Tell me, won't you tell me, tell me, are you brave?

rit.

rit.

It's Such A Good Feeling

(From "MISTER ROGERS' NEIGHBORHOOD")

Words and Music by
Fred Rogers

Duet Part (Student plays one octave higher.)

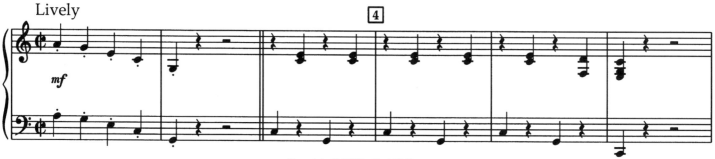

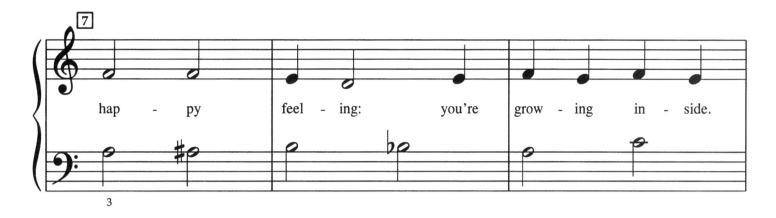

hap - py   feel - ing: you're   grow - ing   in - side.

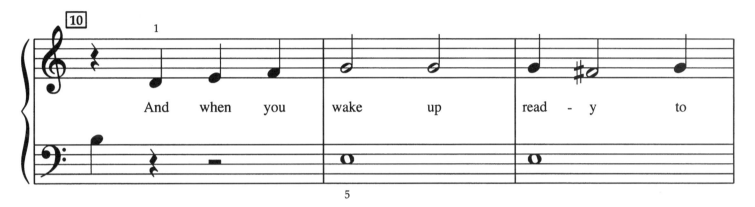

And   when   you   wake   up   read - y   to

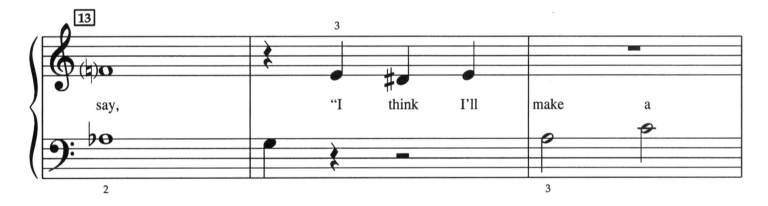

say,   "I   think   I'll   make   a

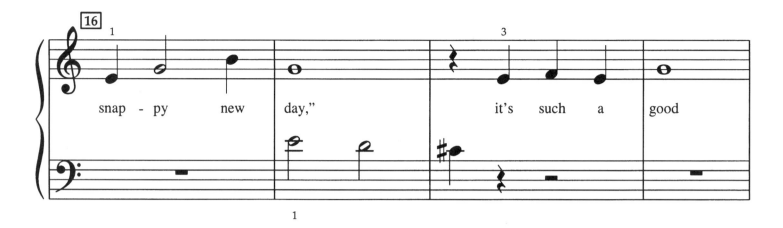

snap - py new day," it's such a good

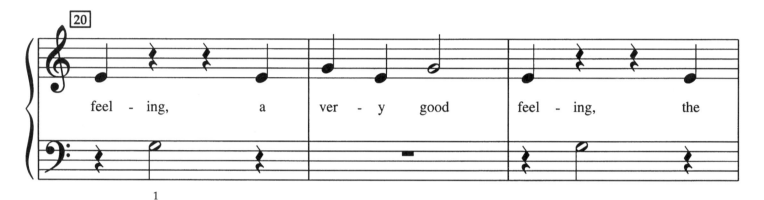

feel - ing, a ver - y good feel - ing, the

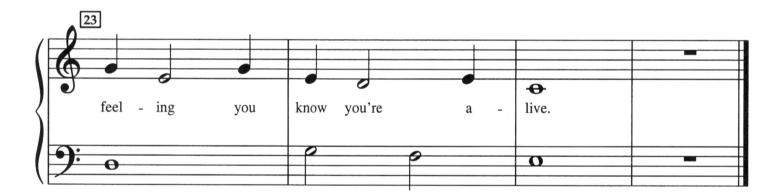

feel - ing you know you're a - live.

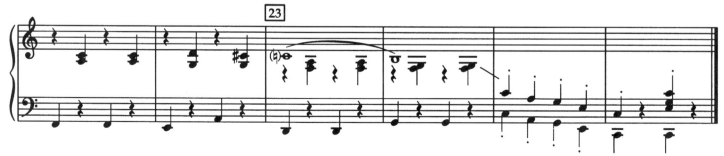

What Do You Do?
(From "MISTER ROGERS' NEIGHBORHOOD")

Words and Music by
Fred Rogers

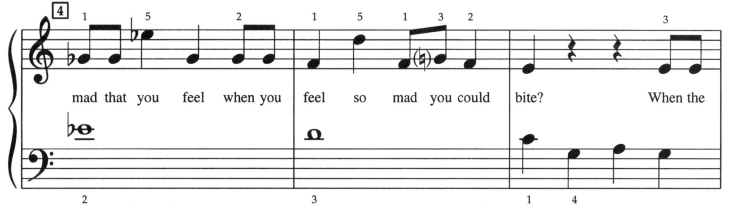

Duet Part (Student plays one octave higher.)

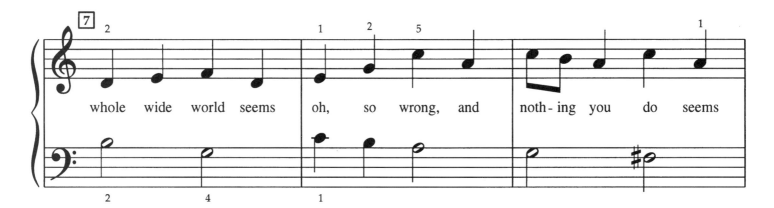

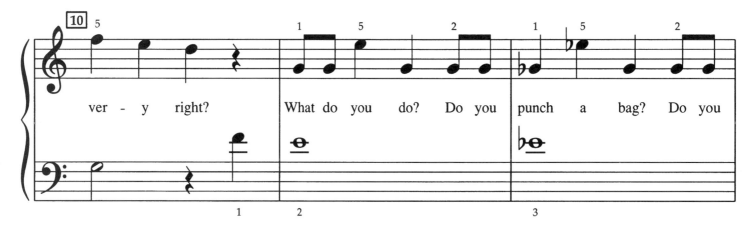

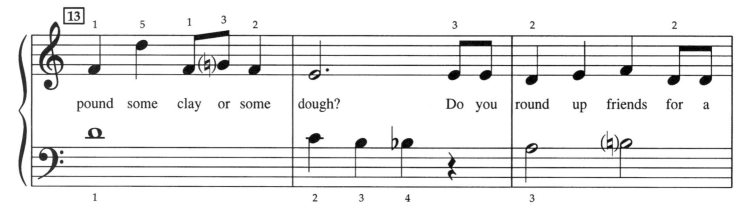

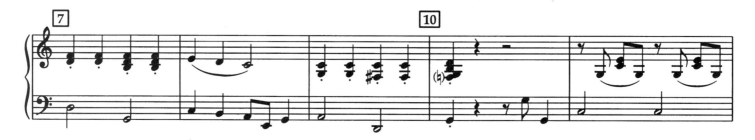

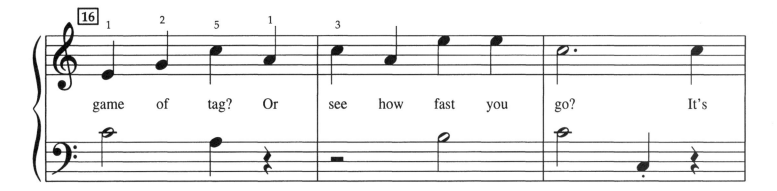

game   of   tag? Or   see   how   fast   you   go?   It's

19 Slower

great to be a - ble to stop   when you've planned a   thing that's wrong,   and   be

21   **Tempo 1**

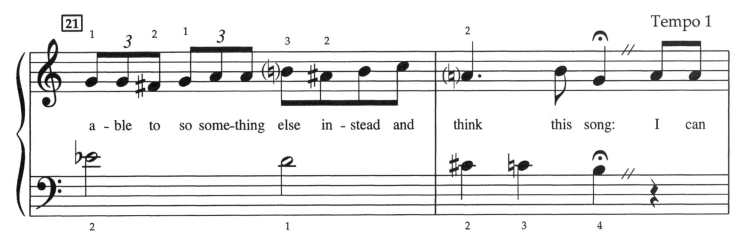

a - ble   to   so some-thing else in - stead and   think   this song: I   can

16

19 Slower   **21**   **Tempo 1**

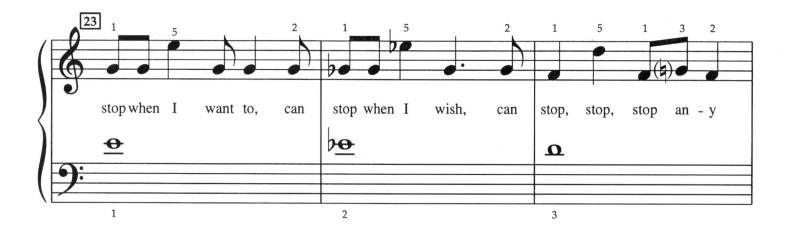

stop when I want to, can stop when I wish, can stop, stop, stop an-y

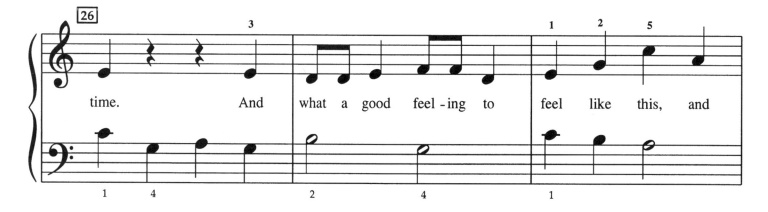

time. And what a good feel-ing to feel like this, and

know that the feel-ing is real-ly mine. Know that there's some-thing

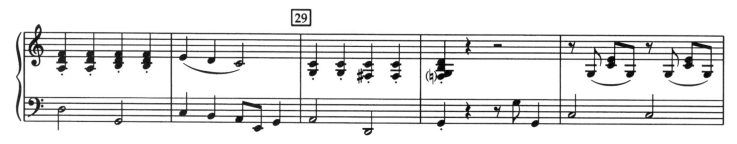

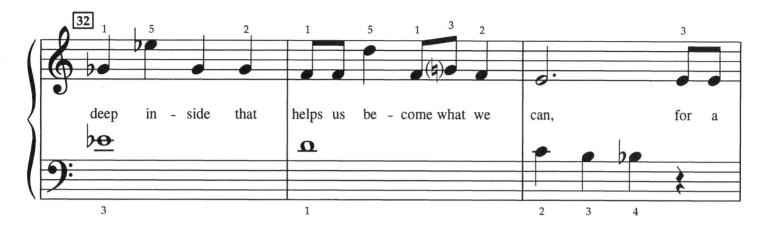

deep in - side that helps us be - come what we can, for a

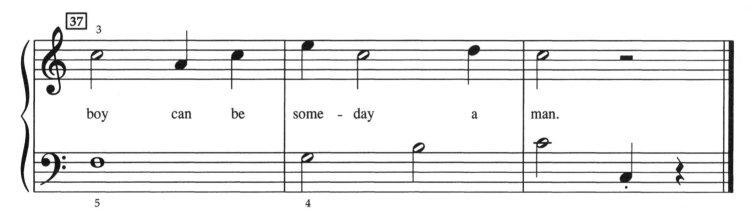

girl can be some - day a wom - an and a

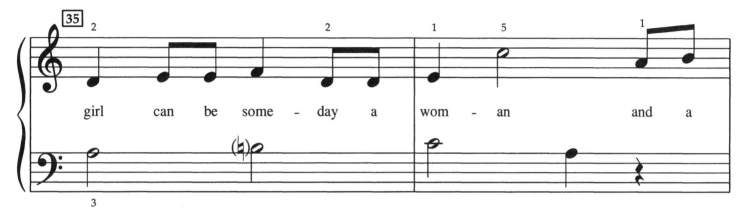

boy can be some - day a man.

Sometimes People Are Good

(From "MISTER ROGERS' NEIGHBORHOOD")

Words and Music by
Fred Rogers

Moderately

Some - times peo - ple are

good, and they do just what they should. But the

Duet Part (Student plays one octave higher.)

Moderately

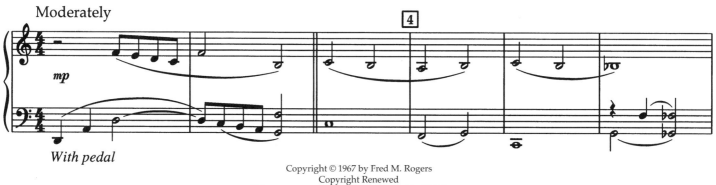

With pedal

ver - y same peo -ple who are | good some -times are the | ver - y same peo -ple who are

bad some - times. It's | fun - ny but it's | true. It's the

same, is - n't it, for | me? Is - n't it the | same for you?

Won't You Be My Neighbor?

(From "MISTER ROGERS' NEIGHBORHOOD")

Words and Music by
Fred Rogers

Duet Part (Student plays one octave higher.)

neigh-bor-ly day for a beau-ty. Would you   be   mine?   Could you   be   mine?   I have

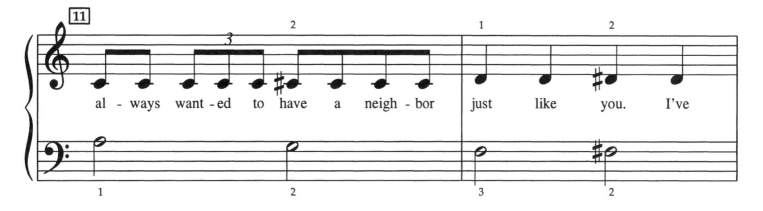

al - ways want -ed to have a neigh - bor   just   like   you.   I've

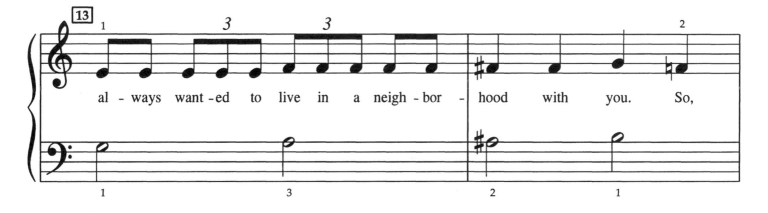

al - ways want -ed to live in a neigh - bor - hood   with   you.   So,

let's make the most of this beau-ti-ful day. Since we're to-geth-er, we might as well say,

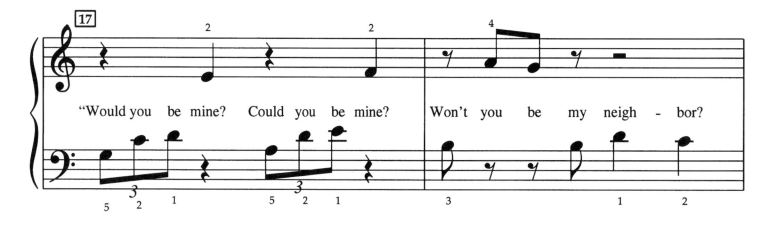

"Would you be mine? Could you be mine? Won't you be my neigh-bor?

Won't you please, won't you please? Please won't you be my neigh-bor?"
rit.

rit.

p

You Can Never
Go Down The Drain

(From "MISTER ROGERS' NEIGHBORHOOD")

Words and Music by
Fred Rogers

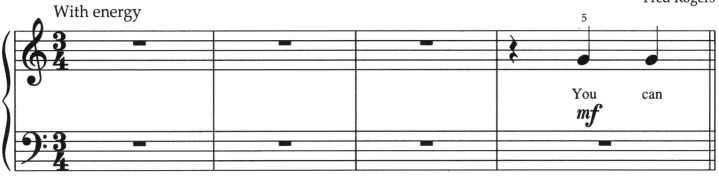

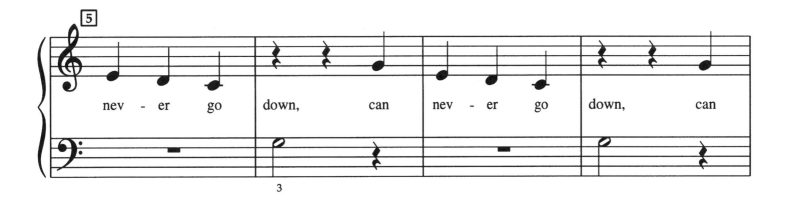

Duet Part (Student plays one octave higher.)

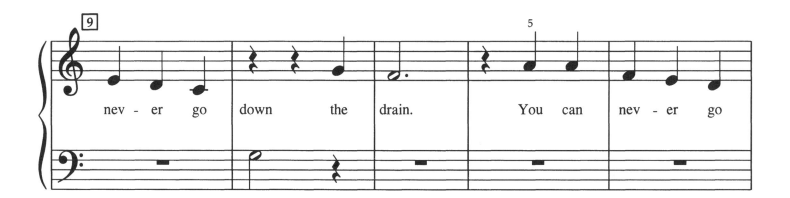

nev - er go down the drain. You can nev - er go

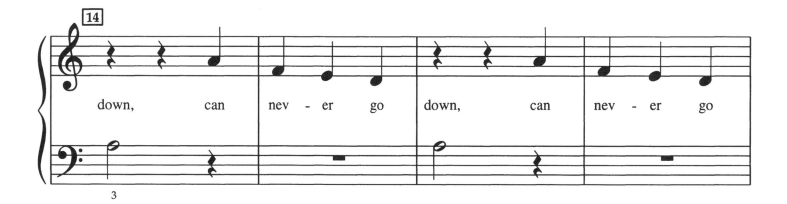

down, can nev - er go down, can nev - er go

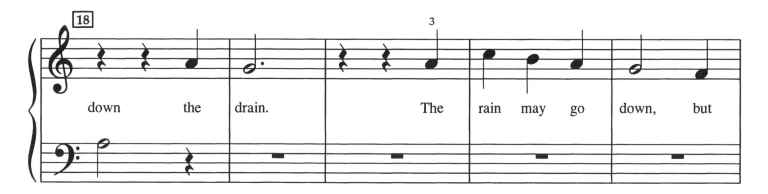

down the drain. The rain may go down, but

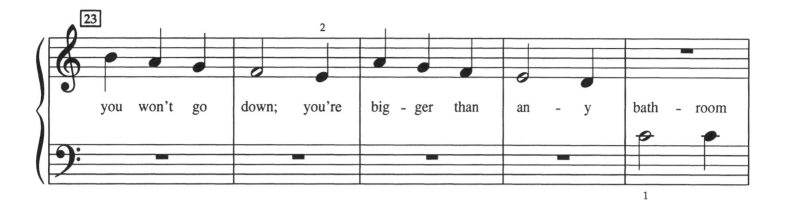

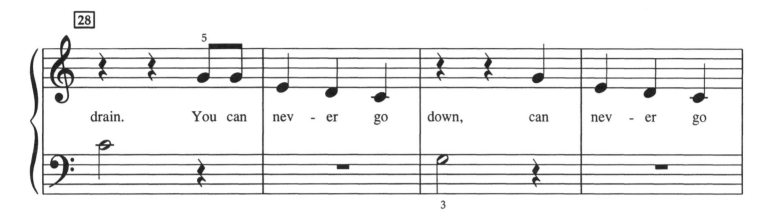

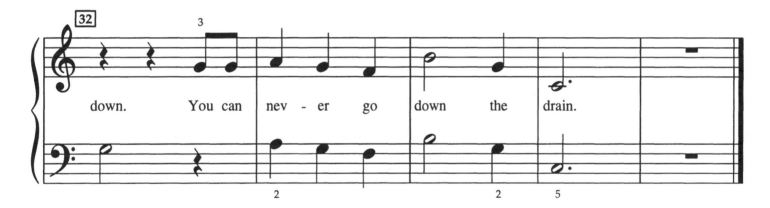

You've Got To Do It
(From "MISTER ROGERS' NEIGHBORHOOD")

Words and Music by
Fred Rogers

You can make be-lieve it hap-pens, or pre-

tend that some-thing's true. You can wish or hope or con-tem-plate a

Duet Part (Student plays one octave higher.)

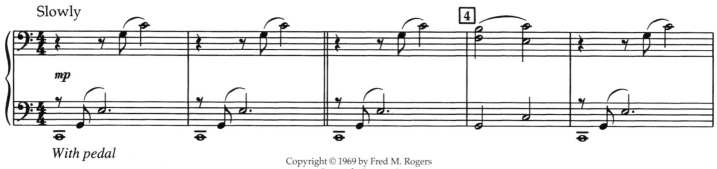

With pedal

thing you'd like to do. But un - til you start to do it, you will

nev - er see it through, 'cause the make - be - lieve pre - tend - ing just won't

a tempo

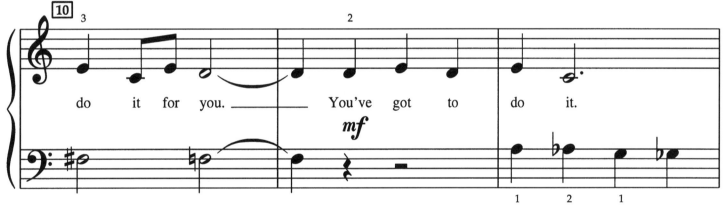

do it for you. _____ You've got to do it.

mf

a tempo

mf

Ev - 'ry lit - tle bit, you've got to   do it,   do it, do it, do

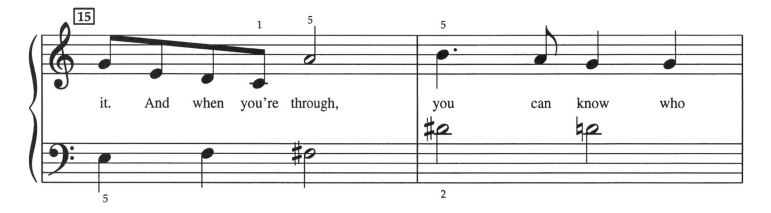

it. And when you're through,   you   can know   who

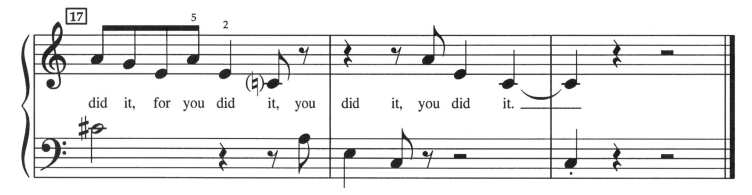

did it, for you did   it, you   did   it, you did   it. ___

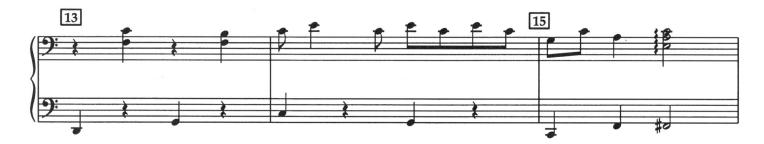

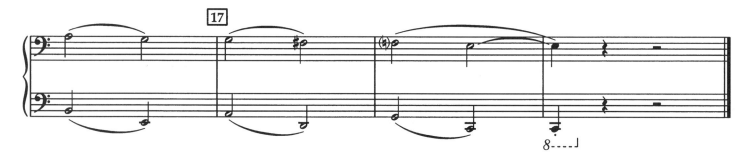